Sacred Soul Simplified

A purposeful pocket companion

Volume 1

SABRINA LISA CLERY

CONTENTS

DEDICATION

My Creator. My Òrìṣà. My Ancestors.
My Ori. My Soul.
My Daughter. My Parents.
My Siblings. My Family. My Teachers.
My Mentors. My Healers. My Loves.
My BFF. My Queens.
My Tribe. My Muse.

ACKNOWLEDGMENTS

There are so many people and experiences that I acknowledge because of how they have shaped me and led to these pages, but there are three people in particular who have directly contributed to each word you will read.

My daughter, Kaya Sky, is my greatest inspiration and teacher. She is my reason and my why. Since the first second I was aware of her presence, she reshaped how I express and emote. To this day, there is no one I talk to more than her — and that started even before I saw her face. So if I am known to have any acumen for speaking and writing, I owe it to my fly Ky Sky. As a single mother, it was essential for me to be as purposeful as I could when speaking to her, since I had no one else consistently around to ensure that I wasn't inflicting harm with my words, especially in the rare moments when I had to reprimand. I am so grateful that in her teens, she calls me her favorite person, so I must be doing something right. I have read so many books to her over the years, and I look forward to reading her the one we wrote together.

My BFF… Melissa Roxanne Duncan-Seon, who combed over every word of this book multiple times to get it ready to publish. This beautiful, brilliant woman and I have had ups and downs since her angel daddy brought us to each other at the age of seven, and today, we stand more solid than I could have ever fathomed. Our bond is a testament to so many *cosmic concepts* addressed in these pages because we have been through so much together and apart. Still, it all always led us back to each other. She is my fig tree, as they have the deepest roots, and I am so excited to see how we continue to grow.

And finally, Mr. Jermain Miller. The man who made this publication possible. Literally. It is hard to put into words how much respect I have for him as I watch him raise three boys as a single father while writing and publishing books. His vision, discipline, dedication, and heart are beyond motivational, and I am truly honored to know him. I remember one of the first conversations we had, and after I shared my perspective, he said, "That's deep…you have to write a book." Well, here it is, and I am so thankful to him for his encouragement and support.

INTRODUCTION

First and foremost, I would like to express my deep gratitude to The Source of Creation... the root from where it all blooms. I had so many ideas and titles in mind for what I wanted to publish, and finally achieved clarity and the guidance to share in deliberate doses. As a result, these succinct pages will serve as Volume 1, inspired by what I practice and preach.

My name is Sabrina Lisa Clery, but I go by SabrinaSahara. I partake in various artistic endeavors, but will simply describe myself with the title that was celestially given to me: Ancestral Alchemist. That title encompasses how I express my creatrix energy guided by my very audible Ancestors. It is my duty to share transmissions from my transitioned tribe that I hope will benefit humanity. I recommend that you read this introduction in its entirety to get a full scope of how these pages can assist your soul's ascension process.

My life's purpose is to translate and transform guidance I receive through various creative and spiritual expressions. My mission is to disseminate the information in straightforward yet uplifting ways to encourage us to stay high vibrational despite the low frequencies that predominate this dense dimension. The highest frequency of love is essential to manifest, and I hope these pages induce the feeling of love required to make our good dreams come true. As a clairaudient, I strive to inspire with the simplified details and downloads I receive about the complex sacred journey of the soul.

This publication shares concise *cosmic concepts* rooted in the law of alignment fundamentals to efficiently elevate our vibrational frequency to shift our subconscious more effectively. This internal transmutation leads to outward transformation that will reflect prosperous and lasting results. My intention is to create a portable reference for self-realization, intuitive revelation, and personal revolution. It is an interactive source from Source that can support us throughout our day and provide cosmic confirmations to what our souls already know.

You will most often come across the reference to "Spirit," which is my way of naming the all-encompassing energy of The Creator/Mother-Father God/Olodumare/The Most High/Youniverse/Source; inclusive of all Light Beings, Starseeds, Sages, Sibyls, Saints, Prophets, Òrìṣà, Netjeru, Angels, Ancestors, Ascended Masters, Gods, Goddesses, Guardians, Spirit Guides, Ancient Kings and Queens, and Divine Deities of all traditions that serve humanity for the highest good of all. Spirit also includes our Ori (Higher Self), for there is no separation. Feel free to fill in Sacred names based on your beliefs, and remember to focus on the message, not the messenger.

Many of these *cosmic concepts* will be familiar to those diving into the soul's sacred journey and they process paranormal paradigms while providing practical perspectives. This aggregation of auspicious abstractions is my attempt to make them easier to incorporate into our daily routine. We are so inundated with the habits of life that we often let our soul work and self-love practices fall by the wayside.

The book's abridged format is uniquely designed to help us carve out even just three minutes to get the guidance our soul seeks most at that moment. The future is now, so we manifest every tomorrow today—because moments are all we truly have to shape the life we want to live. The compact size of the book is also deliberate as it was created to serve as a purposeful pocket companion to have handy for real-time soul support anytime it is needed, especially amidst unexpected challenges. There is also additional information for each *cosmic concept* in the appendix at the end that may resonate on a more personal level.

This book functions as reading material, spiritual guidance, and a divinatory oracle. It provides daily declarations as well as offers soul inquiries and soul work to assist with processing the *cosmic concepts* and your unique resonance with them. Journaling is highly recommended, but the final pages offer space to record your initial reflections on the go. You will also receive many personal downloads as you absorb the messages, so having those pages will increase your chances of implementing the guidance accurately. Aligning with the soul inquiries and soul work at different stages of your life will also provide an in-depth look at your soul's growth and trajectory.

Numerology plays a significant role in life, so it is recommended to research the meaning of the *cosmic concept* numbers and page numbers to receive additional insight. It is also enlightening to delve into your own personal numerology for a deeper perspective into your personality. There are intentionally 33 *cosmic concepts* to honor the master number of divine guidance, creative wisdom, and spiritual ascension, which has sacred symbolism in various spiritual and religious traditions. You will also notice in some *cosmic concepts* that I replace the word "to" with the Roman numeral for the number 2 (II/ii). That change blesses the *cosmic concept* with the intuitive frequency of the master number 11 and the Rastafari term "I and I," which reminds us that we are all connected to all that is.

These pages were put together purposefully but can be read in any order. Like Bibliomancy divination, this book can also provide specific guidance to an inquiry when a page is selected randomly. Don't dismiss a message if it doesn't seem to reference what you inquired about. We often think that we know what is most urgent, but Spirit will always lead us to focus on the issues predominant in our energy field. In these cases, it is especially recommended to complete the suggested soul inquiry and soul work to reveal core concerns that may be a priority to address. Taking the time to explore why something isn't resonating or is triggering can be powerfully enlightening and liberating if you are open to deeper truths about your essence and your experiences.

Each *cosmic concept* will begin with a simple but significant declaration that is easy to memorize. Say it out loud in a command with authority to name and claim the blessing. Repeat it with faith and confidence throughout the day to reprogram your subconscious mind and heal your heart. That is where metamorphosis and magick happen. This practice is extra immersive and transformative when declared in front of a mirror, in the shower/bath, or over water or fruit before consuming. You can bless your water with sea salt and your fruit with cinnamon and honey for extra absorption and abundance.

You can also script the declarations in a journal or notepad, take a picture of it, or whatever makes it easier for you to be reminded of the message(s) as you go through your day. The feeling and faith that you imbue in each declaration will fuel its frequency. You can further accelerate the embodiment of each declaration by concluding with *actualizing activations* such as Àṣẹ, Amen, Ameen, A'ho, Aung, Aum, Abracadabra, It Is Done, So Be It, It's Been, So It Is... Be sure to express your thanks in advance to The Creator and your Ori (Higher Self) to ensure you are in receiving mode. Keep your palms up and open when declaring, affirming, praying, and petitioning to tangibly accept what you are bringing forth. Our palms are portals to everything we wish for our hands to hold.

Each *cosmic concept* also aligns with spiritual and natural associations so you can explore and embrace each message on a holistic level. An accompanying oracle deck is available to facilitate the divination function and for those who love to shuffle like I do. The cards can also be used as a learning tool as they offer an extensive list of associations, which includes chakRAs, Bija (seed) mantras, "I" affirmations, color therapy, Solfeggio frequencies, crystal therapy, Òrìṣà alignment, Archangel alignment, physical and subtle bodies, the elements, essential oils, planetary alignments, days of the week, musical notes, and numbers. My original artwork adorns the book cover and I also share seven of my abstract art pieces, created specifically for the oracle deck, to align with the seven energies embodied in these cards. They provide art therapy as you can use the images to meditate and send concentrated activations to the associated chakRAs. Also known as The Seven Souls of RA, when your chakRAs are aligned, you will naturally live a more balanced and holistic way of life on every level.

When a card or cards are selected, they are presenting calls to action to assist in augmenting your intangible energy to elevate your tangible experiences. When cards frequently repeat or present in reverse, it indicates a need to prioritize working with those areas and alignments. Receive the messages as getting a heads up from Spirit to give that area extra love, attention, and/ or treatment to avoid or alleviate dis-ease. As with the book, the meaning of the numbers on each card selected should be explored to receive additional messages.

It is recommended to take the time to read at least one *cosmic concept* or pull one card daily to maintain the magickal momentum of your soul's union with Source. This consistency will enhance your intuition and expand the synchronicities that will confirm and clarify your everyday choices. Repetition is fundamental for manifesting, so this daily diligence will train your subconscious mind to align with your authentic aspirations. Dive into divine discipline to develop your psychic abilities and eliminate the doubt that can often accompany personal downloads. As we attempt to manifest what is already ours, the work is more in removing resistance, energetic blocks, limiting beliefs and social conditioning so we can be in tune with our Higher Selves & Source. The stuff is just stuff, but must materialize when we are in alignment. The question is, how good do you want it? As you read these *cosmic concepts*, give yourself permission to be everything you are. In doing so, you will become more obedient to the inspired action your soul wants you to take to fulfill its mission and experience an avalanche of abundance.

Thank you in advance for your time and interest in flipping through the purposeful pages of Sacred Soul Simplified - Volume 1. I am honored and grateful that you have chosen to spend these mystical moments with Spirit, with your soul, and with mine.

Sending ancestral love and angelic light. Àṣẹ.

SabrinaSahara

SACRED SUPPLEMENTS

The list below includes items addressed in some of the *cosmic concepts* throughout these pages. These sacred supplements will be useful to have handy, especially if you decide to participate in the soul work suggestions.

Ancestral Altar
Bay Leaves (dried)
Clear Jar or Pot
Cinnamon (ground)
Crystals*
Fireproof Vessel
Frankincense
Fresh Fruit
Grounding Mat
Hamsa
Herbal Tea
Honey
Ice
Journal

Lighter
Mirror
Nazar
Palo Santo
Pen
Permanent Marker
Rose of Jericho (Resurrection Plant)
Sea Salt
Seedling
Soil
Spring Water

---

* Amethyst, Black Obsidian, Black Tourmaline, Carnelian, Citrine, Clear Quartz, Gold Tiger's Eye, Green Aventurine, Lapis Lazuli, Red Jasper, Smoky Quartz, Turquoise

AWARENESS OF ONENESS

"I am you. You are me.
We are one. Youniversally."

We are in awe of celestial bodies above while
often mistreating divine bodies below, including
our own. This happens when we don't fully realize
that we are all interconnected and woven into the
fabric of each other's existence. We are one with
Source, and there can be no separation from that
which we were created from. Everything that
flows from that core of creation is all linked, so
every shift will have an overall consequence. As
planets and moons dance with stars and asteroids
in elliptical orbits, so do we among the same

constellations. We say 'as above, so below' because our inner space mirrors outer space, and the sacred synchronicity of space sets the stage for earthly parallels. Every movement in cosmic tandem reminds us about cause and effect, which is why purposefulness is imperative. Earthly events are designed to be as capricious and mysterious as the celestial ones, so it is up to us to best manage how we engage with whatever life throws our way.

Our choices have an impact on the cosmos. The more we accept the reality that every choice we make can affect our youniverse and others in it, the more mindful and soulful we will be. When we embody that belief, we consider those who are a part of our *true tribe*, and it inspires us to conduct ourselves with integrity and kindness at our core. This also inspires us to honor our ancestors, who I refer to as our *transitioned tribe*. We vibrate higher when we remember that we are a continuation of our ancestors' lives. There is so much below to remind us that we are all one, much like the stars above that we are made up of.

Soul Inquiry:

When are you most reminded that we are all one?

Soul Work:

List ways you can enhance your oneness with Source, your *true tribe,* and your *transitioned tribe.* Act on them.

ChakRA Activation:

Root - Muladhara - Lam - I Am - Red - 396 Hz - Red Jasper

DIVINE DUALITY

*"I am she. I am he. Everything
that is, is found in me."*

Yin, Yang. Up, Down. Hot, Cold. Dark, Light. Good, Bad. In, Out. Top, Bottom. Day, Night.... The list can go on and on because this third density is composed of divine duality. Although we tend to think of them as opposites, the principle of duality teaches us that we are all intricately created with interconnected extremes, so finding balance is key. Those perceived contrasts often present the challenge of choice. Although we may feel two opposite conditions, reality doesn't always make it easy to choose both. That is where reflection and discernment must play active roles before we take action. Once we are in a more neutral vibration, we can prioritize how to proceed and integrate our polarities for an authentic and autonomous existence.

We are perfectly made despite our humanly perceived flaws and contradictions, and embracing our dualistic nature is crucial to embody the essence of our earthly experience. When we choose to make it okay to feel two things that may seem contrary, we allow ourselves to fully explore the complexity of our core. We must stretch ourselves beyond singular thoughts that may stem from ego, conditioning, and obligation and consider compromise to discover our most 'wholistic' self. From that place of self-actualization, we thrive in our paradoxical purpose and expand our lives and the world in innovative ways.

Soul Inquiry:

Does embracing your duality make you uncomfortable? Why or why not?

Soul Work:

Write down your contrasts and list ways you can integrate them. Embrace and embody that whole you.

ChakRA Activation:

Sacral - Svadhishthana - Vam - I Feel - Orange - 417 Hz - Carnelian

THE POWER OF THREE

*"I invoke the power of three to
expand my community."*

Many things happen in threes. Past, Present,
Future. Mind, Body, Soul. Birth, Life, Death.
Beginning, Middle, End. The concept is endless
because the sacred vibration of a trinity evokes
eternity. The power of three is often used in
magick, whether through speaking, scripting, or
ritual, because of its full circle essence that can
swiftly lead to completion and wish fulfillment.
Our individual power should never be denied,
but it can be enhanced by the frequency of three
because of the number's alignment with creation,
the secrets of the cosmos, and the creatrix energy

of divine femininity. Speaking or scripting actualizing activations like Àṣẹ and Abracadabra three times when manifesting can accelerate your intentions.

The number three embodies collective consciousness and amplified energy is emanated when creating collaboratively in community. It intensifies what can be achieved when we come together with like-minded souls for a common goal. We are capable of accomplishing endeavors alone, but imagine the productive possibilities with a unified team. Teamwork provides support, encouragement, motivation, and more hands on deck to tackle tasks. Three people coming together with an inspired intention and productive plan have a spiritual advantage to create something prolific that can steadily expand and leave a legacy.

Soul Inquiry:

Think about two people who you consider to be on your team. How do you show up for each other?

Soul Work:

Script a goal-oriented declaration that can empower and inspire your team. Share it with them so you can all say and script it three times before you start your day to enhance your motivation and productivity.

ChakRA Activation:

Solar Plexus - Manipura - Ram - I Do - Yellow - 528 Hz - Citrine

4

FOUR WALLS OF MANIFESTING

"I align my thoughts, feelings, words, and deeds to manifest my needs."

We all have ideas of what we want and/or need, so we do whatever we can to manifest them into reality. We use various internal and external divinatory tools, spiritual practices, personal skills, professional acumen, and intellectual abilities to experience what starts as a vision. With all that is accessible to call in miracles, we often lose sight of the basic requirements that must work in tandem for the magick to happen. What we think, feel, say, and do to prove that we believe in the inevitability of our desires before they are manifested plays a key role in their materialization.

If we think about these four aspects — feelings, thoughts, words, deeds — as walls, our manifestation is the roof, which can only be built if all four walls are even and solid. If not, the instability of our walls can't sustain the structure of our roof. Our energy is composed of these walls, so we must take the time to ensure that we are in faith-full agreement with what we are manifesting to send consistent messages to the youniverse. As we process our purpose, we must first focus on our fundamental needs and acknowledge where energetic inconsistencies are preventing them from being fulfilled. That's the only way we can get into alignment to ensure we receive all the more in store.

Soul Inquiry:

How much faith do you have regarding receiving a need you are manifesting?

Soul Work:

Visualize something you need. Write down how you feel about it, what you think about it, how you speak about it, and what action steps you are taking to manifest it. How do they align? What inconsistencies arise that should be adjusted to strengthen their alignment?

ChakRA Activation:

Heart - Anahata - Yam - I Love - Green - 639 Hz - Green Aventurine

WINDS OF CHANGE

*"I welcome the winds of change that
come through challenge."*

The wind is ever-changing, unpredictable, illusive, and transient. It is something that moves around us that we can feel, yet cannot hold. The wind has the power to soothe or destroy. It can bring destruction to structures that are not solid to expose necessary changes to rebuild stronger. Change cannot be avoided and is known as the only constant, so it is always in our best interest to expect, accept, and initiate change. When we are able to do that, even sudden shifts are managed with grace and gratitude, which is the most powerful place to manifest from.

Be one with the wind by acknowledging that change often comes on the other side of a challenge. Despite the distress that comes with it, remember that it is not happening *to* you; it is happening *for* you. That inner-standing is the difference between you choosing to be a victim or a victor. Change makes way for metamorphosis, transformation, transmutation, and alchemy, and it helps us get more comfortable with being uncomfortable. The wind can uproot and lift us away from what we know, but we must be grateful for the new places and faces that can only be experienced when we land on higher ground.

Soul Inquiry:

Do you fear change? Why or why not?

Soul Work:

Go outside or be near an open window. Breathe deeply and journal about changes you want to make in your life and an action plan on how to achieve them.

ChakRA Activation:

Throat - Vishuddha - Ham - I Speak - Blue - 741 Hz - Turquoise

6

SIXTH SENSING

"I listen to my intuition to take inspired action."

There is a theory that explains that we have three brains: our intellectual brain, our heart, and our gut. When they are activated simultaneously, we have access to our intuition in a very palpable way. We not only hear our inner voice in logical and emotional ways, but also in the physical sensations and/or warnings that can arise. Pay attention to those. Everyone can tap into that sixth sense, but we too often ignore it or make excuses in order to maintain the status quo. Many people who are not as spiritually sensitive can make us feel foolish for making tangible decisions based on intangible directions. However, don't be externally influenced to take your internal guidance for granted. The more we tune in to those intuitive moments, the more frequent and acute they will become to provide us with protection, prosperity, purpose, and peace.

Spirit will always send signs and signals our way to not just make sure we are safe, but to give us the practice of receiving them and being obedient. The easy part is often receiving the messages, but how we choose to follow through is the real challenge. Perspective also plays a major role in those challenges because we tend to see things the way we want to see them. The Creator granted us free will and the gifts of co-creation/ co-curation, so making choices from an intuitive place makes it easier for us to take inspired action on the options that will truly serve us.

Soul Inquiry:

How do you include your intuition when making practical life choices?

Soul Work:

Close your eyes and think about something you are confused about. Write out what your brain, heart, and gut would say about it. Evaluate how they differ and what they may have in common to help you gain more clarity before making a decision.

ChakRA Activation:

Third Eye - Ajna - Om - I See - Indigo - 852 Hz - Lapis Lazuli

PERFECTLY MADE

"I am perfectly made."

We are conditioned to say that we are not perfect because we align human flaws with imperfection. Despite any perceived mistakes we make, we must not forget that we are made in the image of The Creator, Who is perfection. As a result, we, too, are perfect and just get mired in the dramas and traumas of life that take us out of the natural state in which we entered the world at birth. We could do many things that someone could judge, but that cannot remove the divine spark of perfection we are made of. Part of embodying that essence of perfection is making sure that we revere our relationships, especially our relationships with Self & Source.

Nurturing our dynamics with care and concern is the foundation for healthy exchanges and harmonious encounters. That perfection must be practiced. It is up to us how much consistency we choose to exercise with those who matter most. We are all one of a kind, and every day, we are navigating new life experiences that we did not get trained for. The grace that we are given from Spirit is unconditional, so it is vital that we give ourselves and others grace as well. We will let ourselves and others down at times, but ensuring that we are accountable without beating ourselves up enhances our divine spark. That divine spark reveals to us the fine line between how we show up for others and for ourselves. Leaning into that perfection with humility alleviates the defensiveness or denial that fuels feuds. Finding the balance between being purposeful with others while prioritizing ourselves is perfection.

Soul Inquiry:

How have you been hard on yourself and others for disappointing choices?

Soul Work:

Write letters to yourself and others complimenting the divine spark you see amidst the perceived human flaws.

ChakRA Activation:

Crown - Sahasrara - Ah - I Know - Purple - 963 Hz - Amethyst

INFINITE ABUNDANCE

"I am so grateful that I am infinite abundance."

Abundance is often categorized solely as wealth, and we limit its blessings when we confine it to financial frequencies. As we manifest, we should keep the complete meaning of abundance in mind, commonly defined as an ample amount, and be specific about what we want in abundance. Love, health, peace, protection, and every other high vibrational gift Spirit has for us should also be a part of our abundance aspirations. We want to be aware that Spirit not only has a generous supply of all good things, but an infinite supply. That is why we must never forget that we are worthy enough to name and claim all that we hope to experience and expand in our lives. We may not receive it all exactly as we wish, but that does not wane our worth.

The game changer is not thinking of infinite abundance as something to attain that is outside of us. Abundance is our divine inheritance, to which we all have instant and limitless access. Abundance is something that we are, not something that we can get. The youniversal truth is that Spirit's boundless favor is a guaranteed inheritance once we reprogram ourselves to believe that. "Believe and Receive," as the celestial saying goes. Imagine if we truly left no room for doubt. Your soul, like The Creator, is eternal, and your alignment with infinity is only the beginning of experiencing your infinite abundance.

Soul Inquiry:

What beliefs have created doubt surrounding your infinite supply of abundance?

Soul Work:

Write an "I am" list of everything you wish to experience in abundance and speak it out loud.

ChakRA Activation:

Root - Muladhara - Lam - I Am - Red - 396 Hz - Red Jasper

EMBRACING ENDINGS

"I accept endings to accelerate expansion."

As humans, we tend to struggle with endings because we are wired to think of them as losses. We have a hard time reconciling with not having something or someone that we got used to. We get attached quickly and often feel the need to hold onto things and people, perhaps longer than we should. Not only can that hold us back from what is truly meant for us, but it can also cause us to hinder others from evolving. All of us can think of past examples of not wanting to let go, but in hindsight, we can acknowledge that the ending led to something new. That is why we must embrace endings with a sense of gratitude due to the inevitable expansion they will lead to.

Fortified faith assists us throughout the process and makes the transition so much easier and faster. We often get lost in loss when we are unprepared or ill-equipped for change and when we don't have a holistic understanding of the cycle of death and rebirth. Everything is energy, and energy never dies. It is always transformed. If we focus on what we believe is gone, it is easy to get stuck in low vibrational feelings. In those moments, we must keep in mind that mourning is love enduring, which should be a celebration in itself. Taking time amidst the tears to give thanks for the memories–and for what is yet to be birthed–can offer the healthy closure that many of us need to truly move on.

Soul Inquiry:

Who or what have you "lost" that you are still not at peace with?

Soul Work:

Journal about the person or about the scenario to express the new experiences that have transpired since and give thanks for how it is all related.

ChakRA Activation:

Sacral - Svadhishthana - Vam - I Feel - Orange - 417 Hz - Carnelian

10

GOD WITHIN

*"I have found God within, so I
can never be without."*

There is nothing that The Creator cannot be or
have, and that great "I AM" is within us. That
primordial essence is all-encompassing, and we
have been made in that image. What, then, could
we possibly be without once it is a part of our
destiny? When we fully embody that truth, we
will eliminate the experience of lack in our lives.
We must appreciate what we have already been
blessed with and be grateful for gratitude. That
vibration will open portals within to grant us
even more access to God and unlock superpowers
dormant in our DNA. It is our birthright to

believe and receive. To name and claim. To demand and command. It is that simple.

Unfortunately, we've forgotten and have complicated things. Many religions contribute to that confusion when they teach us to pray up and out when we should be going inward, because that is where God resides. As a result, we have not strayed from Source; we have strayed from Self. Once we come back into alignment with our true selves, we automatically remember that we can never be apart from Source. The more you revere your godliness, the more you will be reminded by The Creator with cosmic confirmations and tangible treats.

Soul Inquiry:

Has religion or spirituality ever made you feel separate from God?

Soul Work:

Write a list of ways you can remind yourself that God resides within you.

ChakRA Activation:

Solar Plexus - Manipura - Ram - I Do - Yellow - 528 Hz - Citrine

11

YOUNIVERSAL LAWS

"I am one with the ever-expanding
youniverse. It is law."

You are a reflection of this vast youniverse, and
your anatomy mirrors the solar system—so take
up space! If the youniverse is ever expanding, so
are you, and so is God! You are a galaxy, and your
potential and reach are boundless. There is even
more void and dark matter, and we can alchemize
it. The negative connotations of darkness result
from dark forces that force their ill intentions and
disregard the youniversal laws. We should focus
on the fact that darkness also has a powerful
positive alignment since most transformation
happens in the dark. We can only see the stars in

the night sky, so don't be afraid of the dark. The dark has its place, and we need it to recognize what's bright, so let your shine permeate the dark and transmute the low to light.

Like dark and light, everything is relative, yet related, in this dense, dualistic dimension. It is all subjective, but we are more than what we currently see. We come from beyond, where purposeful principles override what the matrix mandates. Where there are codes and ethics established from the dawn of time to ensure balance and harmony. These youniversal laws should be fundamental to inspire basic levels of humanity, collective consciousness, and self-awareness. Those virtues are not as prevalent in today's society as they ought to be, pulling us farther away from the youniversal laws. Doing our part to restore the divine order may seem insignificant, but in truth, it alters the earthly realm and our very condition within it. You are the youniverse and have the power to transform it.

Soul Inquiry:

How do you wish to transform the youniverse?

Soul Work:

Research the universal laws and explore how you can put them into practice.

ChakRA Activation:

Heart - Anahata - Yam - I Love - Green - 639 Hz - Green Aventurine

12

ANCESTRAL ALIGNMENT

" I am an ancestor."

Ancestral veneration is a fundamental practice in African, Aboriginal, Native, Eastern and other ancient traditions, but it is often misjudged and undervalued in Western practices. The irony is that the Western prevalence of erecting statues and naming streets and institutions in honor of individuals who have transitioned are all forms of ancestral veneration. It is only more often criticized and feared by mainstream mindsets when it is connected to Indigenous lands and cultures. Reclaim this powerful practice by learning and talking more about your ancestors, speaking their names, pouring libation, and creating an ancestral altar. Providing your ancestors sacred space to share offerings of some of their favorite things — including mementos, meals, fresh water, and flowers — is an ideal way to thank them for their presence and presents.

Aligning with ancestors is a sacred art. It thins the veil to receive direct guidance from them, which can fundamentally benefit your day-to-day life and enhance your intuition to guide yourself. Taking moments of silence to welcome their energy and enlightenment gives you access to the esoteric knowledge of the past, present, and future. Honoring those who made your life possible is also a way to stay connected to yourself because not only are our ancestors a part of us, we are our own ancestors. When we consider past life incarnations, multiple dimensions, and starseed lineages, it is safe to say that many of us have been here before, which makes us living ancestors. Our souls are ancient and our bodies are temples, so we are altars and should make sure to offer reverence to ourselves as we do our ancestors.

Soul Inquiry:

How were you introduced to ancestral alignment, and how has it enhanced your connection with yourself?

Soul Work:

Designate a sacred space or create an altar with pictures and mementos of your ancestors and speak their names. Reflect on the reasons why you honor them so you can exhibit some of those same qualities.

ChakRA Activation:

Throat - Vishuddha - Ham - I Speak - Blue - 741 Hz - Turquoise

MAINTAIN BOUNDARIES

"A No to someone else is a Yes to me."

We all know when someone crosses the line with us, but we don't always say or do anything about it. When we get used to a dysfunctional dynamic, we can become docile and desensitized by the discomfort. We sometimes want to pretend everything is okay, don't want to hurt someone's feelings, or lack the confidence to speak up. We may also want to avoid someone's reaction to our truth, so we become trained to maintain their peace by sacrificing our own. Each time we respond that way, we send a message to others that we not only accept the offenses, but are also comfortable with them. Whoever genuinely loves and respects us will make it clear based on how they adhere to our boundaries, which will also let us know if a relationship is healthy enough to preserve.

Saying no, drawing that line in the sand, or walking away is hard for empathic souls because we are conditioned to serve others. Practicing this *cosmic concept* ensures that our natural inclination to serve doesn't turn us into servants. Maintaining boundaries also leads us to prepare our bodies, hearts, minds, and souls for necessary endings—whether the ending of a toxic habit, unhealthy routine, or an abusive dynamic. When we reclaim our power, not everyone will accept it because they only see their loss of control and the inconvenience of having to be mindful and accountable for their behavior. As a result, they will test our resolve by challenging and contesting our newfound strength, and it is up to us to follow through with our convictions. There are risks to everything in life, and navigating our boundaries forces us to face the risk of losing someone else or losing ourselves.

Soul Inquiry:

Who/what do you have difficulty saying 'no' to? Change the perspective and focus on how you can say 'yes' to you.

Soul Work:

Write letters to relevant parties expressing your new boundaries. Share them if/when you are ready, but most importantly, show them.

ChakRA Activation:

Third Eye - Ajna - Om - I See - Indigo - 852 Hz - Lapis Lazuli

14

REGARD YOUR REGRETS

*"I am proud that there are past
choices that I wouldn't repeat."*

As we journey through life, we often have difficulty giving ourselves grace for past choices that we describe as regrets or mistakes. Unfortunately, we forget that every choice we made led us to who we are now and that we had reasons for making those choices. All our experiences shaped and molded our current state and sense of self. More than likely, those choices also made us stronger and more enlightened. That is why I believe that we should regard our regrets. They are tangible evidence of our growth and serve as confirmation of what we wouldn't do again. Every decision we make brings us closer to the best version of ourselves once we choose to be honest and learn from previous choices.

Holding on to something unfortunate that happened in the past allows it to keep happening in the present, which can then make it happen again in the future. Instead, focus on the lessons you have learned through all your reactions and retaliations. Be grateful for how they have contributed to the newfound wisdom that inspires you to respond to life more authentically. That perspective can lead you to the realization that you, in fact, have nothing to regret. It was all meant for you to experience, and it also makes it possible for you to help others avoid certain pitfalls. The reality is that we will make more choices our future self may wish we didn't make, so expect the feeling of regret—but regard it as a requirement for your rise.

Soul Inquiry:

Process some things you consider regrets and the reasons you chose them at the time.

Soul Work:

Verbally forgive yourself for anything you regret while thanking yourself for the lessons you learned.

ChakRA Activation:

Crown - Sahasrara - Ah - I Know - Purple - 963 Hz - Amethyst

ROOTS AND FRUITS

"I am patient with my hidden roots
so I can harvest ripe fruits."

Our aspirations are like seeds that we plant and cultivate through our intentions and actions so they can grow. We often have more than one aspiration, so we are constantly planting many seeds simultaneously, but nature knows when it is time for those seeds to come to fruition. Fruition means ripe and ready so we can enjoy the most succulent version of our desire. Bitter fruits are never as enjoyable, so it will always be worth it to allow for the extra time needed to ensure a delectable experience. It is no different for our aspirations, so appreciate the natural order of things that will guarantee the greatest growth.

Prioritize patience and perseverance to give your roots the time they need to germinate. The longer the time, the stronger and deeper the roots, which will provide longevity to your manifestation instead of risking it being uprooted as quickly as it came. Once that logic lands, you will start to be grateful for nature's perfect pace, raising your vibration to reflect the timeline you wish to experience. It would also be overwhelming to have everything we've planted ready for harvest all at once since what has ripened would be at risk of neglect and spoilage. Just as it takes time and diligence to plant and nurture a seed, it takes that same work ethic to sort through and pick what has grown. Let nature take its course and be thankful for the purposeful progression that will make it easier for you to reap everything you have sown.

Soul Inquiry:

What do you feel you have been waiting a long time for? Isn't it worth the wait?

Soul Work:

Plant a seedling in a clear glass or pot. Nurture and monitor its growth. Align that process and patience to all your growing aspirations.

ChakRA Activation:

Root - Muladhara - Lam - I Am - Red - 396 Hz - Red Jasper

16

SIGNED. SEALED. DELIVERED

"Signed. Sealed. Delivered. It's mine!"

The power of penmanship is underestimated. Scripting your goals, ambitions, plans, desires, and wishes is like your hand picking up a magick wand and decreeing it all into tangible form and lived experience. Your handwriting on paper creates a spiritual covenant, so it is wise to be purposeful about what you write down. The act of scripting gives your words life, which naturally can be effective for any intention. We are literally *spelling* with every letter we write, creating powerful spells with every sentence. Scripting is like drafting a contract with yourself, so be sure to sign your name below the positive promises you pen. Not only does this simple act bind you with your inspired intentions, but it also convinces the subconscious mind to accept the terms of the deal without doubt or delay.

Your signature creates a pact between you and your Higher Self. What you inscribe now becomes an official agreement–leaving no room to question its validity. Given the potency of the handwritten word, there is an added immense power in the unique motif of your signed name. The way you intuitively designed the scripting of your name is a distinct visual representation of your autonomy and your accord. We witness the value we place on a famous person's signature, so we should elevate our own. When you see yourself as the star that you are and augment your signature to autograph status, you will imbue your script with the energy of celebrity. Then, prepare to welcome the abundance, luxury, and opulence that you as well deserve. What's yours is yours, and there is enough for everyone.

Soul Inquiry:

How do you feel about your signature/autograph?

Soul Work:

Sign your name over and over again until you feel a fluidity and power in its presence. Conclude all your sacred scripts with your signature while saying the declaration out loud.

ChakRA Activation:

Sacral - Svadhishthana - Vam - I Feel - Orange - 417 Hz - Carnelian

TOO SACRED TO SHARE

"Some things are just too sacred to share."

On this spiritual journey, we encounter divine intervention and practical magick. Some have become daily occurrences that we are accustomed to, while sometimes our minds are blown. These are moments when we have to discern what should be shared. It can be powerful to share something with select people or the public in order to breathe more life into it. Some things, however, should be protected or kept private until it is the right time to reveal them to ensure their divinely timed fruition. This also applies to creative and professional endeavors, as it is often just as important to keep what you are building under wraps until it is finalized.

Unfortunately, some people don't always have the best intentions for you or your ambitions. They could emit negativity towards your goals, take credit for your ideas, or strategically sabotage them if they are privy to plans or partnerships before they are secure. Sometimes, it is not even intentional, but their envy or jealousy can still be transmitted energetically. Some of the people closest to us are simply naysayers because they are undisciplined and unmotivated. They can have a knack for convincing others that they will not succeed and it is detrimental to believe in someone else's lie rather than your own truth. Your motivation and momentum could be at stake simply by sharing something with the wrong person or at the wrong time, which could pause or prevent your progress. Know when to manifest in silence until your magick is ready for the world.

Soul Inquiry:

What are some experiences or plans that you are hesitant to share?

Soul Work:

Diligently work in silence towards whatever you feel especially inspired about. When you process the necessary discernment, pay close attention to who comes to mind and why.

ChakRA Activation:

Solar Plexus - Manipura - Ram - I Do - Yellow - 528 Hz - Citrine

18

SOVEREIGN SOUL

"I have the power to yay or nay whatever they say."

There are so many ways that we can feel out of control in this capricious world, which often makes us feel powerless. It is especially during these times that we need to remind ourselves that what we feel and think are what multiply, magnify, and manifest. The "powers that once were" have created a global system to condition us to believe that we are not autonomous in attempts to make us feel like they are in control. That belief reaps a resonance that attracts relationships and realities that restrict and restrain us. It also trains us to relinquish our power and allow others to make decisions for us. There is so much more than the world they manipulate, so we should remember that our essence is beyond it and must not consent to their submissive simulation. They are aware that a new era has arrived, so it is time for us to acknowledge the split and accept the transfer of power.

Their desire to dictate will deepen before their dismantling, so we must choose courage and compassion to make our own healthy and humane decisions for the good of all left standing. Our Ori (Higher Self) allows everything meant for us to come through and protects us from what is not, so give thanks for that personal protection. Whether institutional or interpersonal, we must be aware of who is attempting to impede our freedoms. It is only when we reclaim our power and embody our soul sovereignty that we will experience the liberation that is youniversal law. Once we stop complying with repressive regulations, we render self-proclaimed rulers powerless and restore our rights.

Soul Inquiry:

How have you relinquished your power to others?

Soul Work:

Create an action plan to respond with more courage and compassion when you feel powerless.

ChakRA Activation:

Heart - Anahata - Yam - I Love - Green - 639 Hz - Green Aventurine

WATER WORKS

*"I charge the water around and
within me to define my destiny."*

It is a scientific fact that our bodies are mostly
made up of water. Many of us are also aware
that water holds memory. When we combine
these truths, we realize that water can be a potent
element of nature to help manifest the things we
want to flow into our lives. The notion of "my
cup runneth over" comes to mind when thinking
about the benefits of being in a vibration of self-
love, giving, and receiving. We must ensure that
we pour into ourselves first and let others drink of
the overflow while also being discerning enough
to pour where we are watered. Nature cannot

grow or survive without water — including us — so it is imperative to acknowledge and appreciate its medicinal and magickal necessity.

Water cools and cleanses us while having the power to provide clarity, catharsis, and closure. With that knowledge comes many ways we can work with water to manifest. We can increase the current of our currency by saying money affirmations over flowing water, like while in the shower, washing dishes, under the rain, or near a body of water. We can honor divine timing by declaring patience over ice and then drinking the water once the ice has melted. We can even manifest perfect health by speaking to the water within us with unwavering faith. We were gestated in water, we are made up of water, and it is in the very air we breathe. Use every drop to define your destiny.

Soul Inquiry:

What thoughts and feelings do you process (therefore manifest) while in the shower or bath?

Soul Work:

Create your own declarations and speak them over water, ice, herbal tea, and fruit, as well as while pouring libation, washing dishes, watering plants, doing laundry, near bodies of water, in the shower/bath, or when it's raining.

ChakRA Activation:

Throat - Vishuddha - Ham - I Speak - Blue - 741 Hz - Turquoise

20

BURN BABY BURN

"I burn away what can no longer stay."

Fire is a profound purifier due to its alignment with transmutation. When we think about the powerful symbolism of the phoenix rising from the ashes, we are reminded that we can transform into a new state when the old is burned away. Seeing something go up in flames brings a sense of finality due to the rapid destruction that an enveloping blaze causes, yet is ironically the catalyst for metamorphosis. Fire is an intense element primarily because of the pain associated with burning. As a result, many of us have a negative relationship with fire, which hinders us from appreciating the element enough to work with it. Anyone who has experienced a physical burn vividly remembers that excruciating sensation that often takes a long time to heal and can leave scars. We even refer to horrible life experiences or relationships as getting "burned."

The smoke that accompanies fire is also dangerous and can cause us harm. That is why when working with fire, it is imperative to be careful to ensure your safety, that of your loved ones, and your environment. Despite these necessary precautions, healing our apprehension towards fire removes internal and external obstacles from our path to smooth the road toward our destiny. Fire rituals, like burning herbs, barks, incense, resin, candles, or burning letters of release, bring expedited resolutions to our petitions and rekindle our passions. Flame gazing is a powerful way to honor the element of fire and expresses our gratitude for what we're intending to transmute.

Soul Inquiry:

What stagnant feelings, thoughts, environments, and/or dynamics do you wish could just go up in flames?

Soul Work:

Write a list of all you wish to burn away that no longer fits the future vision you see for yourself. Go outdoors and safely burn the list with a dried bay leaf within three days of a full moon. Give thanks to the flame and the smoke as if it is officially done. Discard the cooled ashes as an offering to the wind.

ChakRA Activation:

Third Eye - Ajna - Om - I See - Indigo - 852 Hz - Lapis Lazuli

21

EXHALE. INHALE.
EXHALE

"I exhale the old to inhale the new."

Without breath, our lives would cease, yet it is the most underrated detail of our everyday lives due to how unconscious the act of breathing is. Not being able to breathe or feeling the air being sucked out of a room is the surest way to cause panic, although it doesn't lead us to acknowledge that life force as we should. The simple act of giving thanks for your breath upon waking could make the difference between how we appreciate every experience, good, bad, or ugly, because at least we are still alive to experience it. Tuning into our breath is an expansive and consistent form of gratitude and self-love, as it reminds us to be in sync with the moment and with life itself.

Breathwork is not only a spiritual and meditative practice. It serves as a practical regulator for the body that can attract and influence your experiences. We are accustomed to being guided to first take a deep breath in and then out to get into alignment. Allow me to introduce a breathing exercise I do when performing "Release II Increase" rituals. Instead of beginning with an inhale, start by exhaling all the air from your lungs through your mouth. This assists in clearing all the stale air to make room for your lungs to take in their full capacity of fresh air. When you are ready to inhale, do so from your nose. Exhale through your mouth again and repeat the pattern. Visualize what you want to release with every exhale and what you want to increase with every inhale. Intentionally engage with the Breath of Life to balance your emotions and activate your intentions.

Soul Inquiry:

How have you taken your breath for granted and how can you implement a more conscious connection with your breath on a daily basis?

Soul Work:

Go outdoors or by an open window and perform the breath/visualization exercise described above for three minutes before performing any "Release II Increase" rituals, especially during the week of a full moon.

ChakRA Activation:

Crown - Sahasrara - Ah - I Know - Purple - 963 Hz - Amethyst

22

SOLE II SOIL

"I put my soles to the soil to ground my soul."

One of the best ways to supply overall healing to the mind, body, heart, and soul is by grounding. Putting the bare soles of our feet on soil provides a realignment with the electricity present in our bodies, the Earth, and the cosmos. Also known as earthing, becoming one with our planet is magickal and tangibly replenishing on every level. A sense of being rooted can give us instant access to clarity and the closure needed to make balanced choices.

Grounding can clear blockages and tension and bestow calm, equilibrium, and wisdom.

The consistent practice can draw out negativity and dis-ease by neutralizing the ailments to the Earth. Sometimes, we can feel overwhelmed, and grounding can provide that quick fix to make us feel steady again. That feeling of security and safety assists us in building solid foundations and choosing stable relationships, which helps our manifestations materialize faster. Earthing reminds us that matter matters so that we can balance practicality and spirituality. It is also the perfect time to give thanks to Earth Mother for all she is removing that no longer serves you so you can anchor, ground, and root into your most abundant timeline.

Soul Inquiry:

What circumstances and/or relationships do you wish felt more stable?

Soul Work:

Go outdoors and ground your feet. If not possible, consider getting an electric grounding mat. Give thanks to Earth Mother as you meditate on your fundamental needs. When you are ready, share your truth with those involved.

ChakRA Activation:

Root - Muladhara - Lam - I Am - Red - 396 Hz - Red Jasper

23

BACK II NATURAL

"Time to get back II natural."

Since 2020, life has changed dramatically on a global scale, and we realize now how quickly things shifted. We had no idea of the lasting impact it would have on our sovereignty and autonomy. Hindsight is indeed 20/20, and now that we look back to that time, we can pinpoint many contributing factors to the current state of the world and the grand design of those pulling the strings. Throughout the literal isolation, I remember how incessantly I heard people say that they can't wait for things to get "back to normal." That made me realize that this sense of "normal" is what got us in the mess in the first place. I discovered what was actually needed was for us to get b*ack II natural*; so I coined the term as my professional brand and personal lifestyle.

The practice of getting *back II natural* is the missing link necessary for living our soul's purpose as organic beings. Miracles will be a daily occurrence despite ill intentions once we reroot to the Earth and align with the supernatural. Then, we will be reminded that nature nurtures and provides us with everything we need to survive and thrive. Our realignment with the forces of nature returns us to the fundamental truth that we are nature as well as the stewards of the Earth. It is our responsibility to also take care of our planet as much as we take care of ourselves and each other. We will then have more chances to see and feel the tangible blessings often bestowed upon us by Mother Nature, and synchronicities will accelerate to expand our awareness of oneness and propel our manifestations.

Soul Inquiry:

How does your daily routine and/or environment make you feel disconnected from nature?

Soul Work:

Implement a nature-based practice daily that brings you closer to nature all year round. Stop and smell the roses. Stand under the sun. Appreciate the changing colors of the leaves. Acknowledge the divine design of a snowflake.

ChakRA Activation:

Sacral - Svadhishthana - Vam - I Feel - Orange - 417 Hz - Carnelian

24

RELEASE II INCREASE

"I release all that hinders my increase."

Many of us are conditioned to hold on to things due to a collective scarcity mentality taught by society and sometimes by our parents. This passed-down mindset often results from not having enough or due to experiences of loss. Many of us also fear change and letting go of what is familiar, even if the familiar doesn't feel good. We avoid starting over and stepping outside our uncomfortable "comfort zones" due to uncertainty. These patterns not only expose us to low vibrations, but they risk us attracting more of the same. We stay in depleting dynamics, especially when denial and cognitive dissonance prevent us from seeing when someone is a detriment to our destiny.

We should welcome the disappointments that can assist in releasing any illusions we may have, which can lead us to a more profound sense of clarity about our relationships. If we have a clear vision of who and where we want to be, we must begin to put our ideas and ideals into tangible practice. Timing is divine, but the future is now so heed the urge to purge. We must pluck weeds before we plant seeds for our harvest to be healthy, and it is no different as we plant seeds for our life purpose. So much can grow when we make room to bloom, but we often choose people who bury our bounty, which hinders our heights. Despite the knowledge that there can only be rebirth after death, we often want to avoid the mourning required for our manifestations. Only upon liberating ourselves from the frequency of lack can we accept what we need to release to ensure our increase.

Soul Inquiry:

What/who are you holding on to that you have outgrown?

Soul Work:

Write a list of whatever you feel is not in alignment with your future self and start implementing the necessary changes today.

ChakRA Activation:

Solar Plexus - Manipura - Ram - I Do - Yellow - 528 Hz - Citrine

FEEL IT II HEAL IT

"I must feel it II heal it."

No one enjoys experiencing hurt, pain, heartache, grief, or any emotion that creates a sense of despair. On our spiritual journey, we do our best to ensure we feel the opposite and stay high vibrational to manifest our heart's desires. The reality, however, is that we do exist in a dimension of duality that has ups as well as downs. There will be unavoidable experiences that are unfavorable and we wish we didn't have to endure, but it would be more detrimental to deny them. I firmly believe that all experiences can benefit us — whether good, bad, or ugly — and it is up to us to maintain a balanced

93

perspective to benefit from whatever comes our way. The uncomfortable emotions may make us want to run away or control them, but that only leads to more problems over time.

The adage that time heals all wounds has its place, but it works best if we face our feelings and observe what may be needed to mend. That practice requires emotional intelligence and vulnerability. When we take the time to tune into our hearts and feel what we are going through, we can observe various issues that arise. We will be able to fully process what has triggered those emotions and then figure out why it has inspired those feelings. From there, more questions can be addressed internally to help us make sense of our external responses, reactions and retaliations. We are often triggered by something or someone rooted in something or someone else, so taking the time to be honest about how we really feel can lead to healing much deeper than anticipated and help us manifest more effectively.

Soul Inquiry:

How have you avoided unfavorable feelings?

Soul Work:

Take the time to process situations that make you feel hurt. Script and speak your raw emotions to help you heal.

ChakRA Activation:

Heart - Anahata - Yam - I Love - Green - 639 Hz - Green Aventurine

FACE IT II REPLACE IT

"I will face it II replace it."

This concept works hand in hand with the previous one because we must first face our feelings to heal them, which leads us to figure out what needs to be replaced. We all have patterns often led by our emotions, especially when we don't take the time to process those emotions. Once we have journeyed through the feel and the heal, a level of clarity and closure can be attained. It can then become easier to acknowledge what changes we need to make to avoid repeating self-defeating tendencies. Once in that augmented alignment, we are more equipped to protect our energy and preserve our peace.

It is up to us to decide how much we allow an external experience to negatively impact our emotions. A true sense of emotional balance can be achieved when we honestly navigate that internal challenge, and then a more solid sense of self can emerge. The process takes time, practice, and discipline, but eventually, that new version of us cannot be emotionally triggered in the same way, even if the same unfavorable thing happens — even if by the same person. We can now be in full control of our responses due to a deeper inner-standing of response-ability. The ability to respond versus react or retaliate happens more easily when we are responsible about how we really feel and what we need to heal due to the brave choice to face what we know we should replace.

Soul Inquiry:

How have you allowed external experiences to negatively impact your emotions?

Soul Work:

List what changes you can make to be more response-able in triggering situations and implement them when challenges arise.

ChakRA Activation:

Throat - Vishuddha - Ham - I Speak - Blue - 741 Hz - Turquoise

27

EYE SEE YOU

"When I claim a curse, I curse myself."

Magick is as real and as effective as the person using it, which also means that magick can be used based on the intentions of each individual. As a result, we can be susceptible to negative forces if targeted by someone with negative intentions. There are references made in the spiritual community regarding black magick, evil eye, generational curses, ancestral wounds, and spiritual bondages that can be passed down through bloodlines and incarnations. Whether we refer to them as a curse, hex, or spell, the thought of them having some controlling force over our lives and families can be scary and defeating. The key word, however, is *thought*. Our imagination is where real results begin, so we should try to only entertain the thoughts that we want to manifest into matter. It is for this reason that I do not subscribe to the idea that any external ill intention can influence my destiny more than my internal inspired intention.

That doesn't mean that someone cannot have the inclination to attempt the negative pursuit, but we do have a choice to give it power over our own will. We should align with the unwavering faith in our divine protection and favor that anoints us without fail. We must also trust in our own ability to see beyond our two eyes when something doesn't feel right so that we can neutralize any negativity and return to sender if necessary. Everything is intangible energy and takes time to land in tangible form, so declare "eye see you" to any malefic energies that dare so they are duly warned before they expose themselves to the ricochet of your providence.

Soul Inquiry:

How have you been negatively impacted by thoughts or stories of dark magick being used against you and/or your family?

Soul Work:

Declare "eye see you" to rebuke all negative narratives. They are no longer your story. Cleanse yourself, your home, and personal spaces you frequent with Palo Santo and/or frankincense and take a weekly spiritual bath with sea salt.

ChakRA Activation:

Third Eye - Ajna - Om - I See - Indigo - 852 Hz - Lapis Lazuli

28

MIRROR WORK

"I revel at my own reflection."

We tend to forget how magickal we are as we navigate this mundane matrix. We look up at the stars at night and revel at how wondrous they are, yet we don't recognize our own reflection in them. We are made of star stuff, and it is only when we truly see ourselves the way we see the stars that we will fully shine. This journey is not about seeking and finding the Self. It is about remembering and returning to the Self. A powerful way to do that is by looking at our reflections in the mirror first thing in the morning to come face to face with our natural self. A mirror is the only way we can see a clear representation of the Self and the

Soul. The eyes are the windows to the soul, so it is when we take time in front of a mirror to gaze into our own eyes, the way we gaze at the stars, that we can discover the depths of our destiny.

Mirror work is an emotive and cathartic self-love practice where you say affirmations, declarations, and compliments while looking at yourself. Speak freely to remind yourself of all you have accomplished and conquered. Proclaim that you don't look like what you've been through. Congratulate yourself for your perceived wins, and be gentle with yourself for your perceived losses. Be proud of everything you think you did right, and forgive yourself for everything you think you did wrong. Take it up a notch by standing naked in front of a full-length mirror and compliment every part of your body. You are perfect, so love the skin you're in and witness the galaxies in your reflection.

Soul Inquiry:

What is your internal self-talk when you see your reflection first thing in the morning?

Soul Work:

Stand in front of a mirror and implement any of the suggestions above that resonate with you.

ChakRA Activation:

Crown - Sahasrara - Ah - I Know - Purple - 963 Hz - Amethyst

29

GROWING PAINS

"I welcome the grind that comes with the growth."

No pain, no gain. That's what they say, right? Although I don't believe that we can only gain through pain, I do acknowledge that there are so many blessings and lessons on the other side of hardship. Change often comes through challenge, and our achievements wouldn't have as much value if they were easy to attain. If we attempt to reach a mountain peak, we expect it to be arduous and require a clear vision, discipline, resilience, and specific equipment and training. Every step will get harder before it gets easier because our muscles will ache, but we will only get stronger if we don't give up.

This mountain climbing analogy relates to life and all we encounter as we grind to achieve specific altitudes. Life is about growth because every day that we are blessed to breathe, we are one day older and wiser. Each new day grants us the privilege to climb to new heights, and every step demands dedication. Procrastination threatens your purpose, so committing to yourself, your gifts, your goals, and your vision requires consistency, which rarely comes easily. Along with passion comes pain when we go through rejection, loss, and setbacks that make us feel like we're starting from scratch. Those overwhelming experiences can feel like we've hit rock bottom, but those who have a harder path have a higher purpose. There is so much power in knowing that we can climb any mountain, but remember that we also have the power to build mountains as we climb.

Soul Inquiry:

When have you experienced such a hardship that it made you give up on someone or something?

Soul Work:

Strategize how you can recommit to someone or something you quit that still holds a healthy place in your heart.

ChakRA Activation:

Root - Muladhara - Lam - I Am - Red - 396 Hz - Red Jasper

30

SHADOW AND SHINE

"I accept my shadow and accentuate my shine."

There are many facets to us that are necessary to navigate this dense, dualistic dimension. Through self-study, we are often faced with aspects of ourselves that are seemingly contradictory. These contrasts mirror opposing energies, entities, emotions, expressions, environments, and experiences that we encounter daily. They can exhibit as making choices that go against a moral, value, promise, or expectation that may cause us to question our integrity. Although it is imperative to prioritize treating ourselves and others with fairness and respect, there are moments when we will disappoint. Through processing the dissonance and the drama that may ensue from the discord, we can be accountable and apologetic without feeling guilt or shame. Give yourself grace by acknowledging the discomfort and compassion you could only feel because of your good conscience. In turn, try to grant others that same grace and forgiveness, especially when they attempt to make amends.

As we walk in the light, there will be moments when our darkness will be explored. It is not weakness, but, in fact, realness, and you may be faced with those contrasts so you can be sure of the choices you wish to make. Reflect on the inconsistencies, and be honest with yourself while taking stock of the risks and rewards to avoid being reckless. It is bittersweet to acknowledge that your authenticity may lead you to betray another to be true to yourself. Still, you will always be lying to someone if you are lying to yourself. When you face your shadow, you are reminded that the light always has your back, so accept your shadow as you accentuate your shine to make choices that you can stand by.

Soul Inquiry:

How do you process and accept contradictory feelings and/or actions?

Soul Work:

Reflect on a choice that was influenced by your shadow. Clear any guilt or shame by writing out what it taught you and how it has added to your shine. Safely burn the page(s) if privacy is paramount; it will also help transmute the energy.

ChakRA Activation:

Sacral - Svadhishthana - Vam - I Feel - Orange - 417 Hz - Carnelian

31

THERE ARE NO DILEMMAS

"If I don't know, the answer is No."

We often find ourselves at a crossroads when weighing different options. When we feel unsure of which path to take, we consider that a dilemma. Dilemmas can be unsettling because we are presented with multiple unclear choices. What we often don't do when processing dilemmas is realize that not making a choice is also an option, and that it is not in anyone's best interest to make a decision when in doubt. You have the right to 'just say no' to all the options you are uncertain about. It is also important to question your choices and be honest about the root of them.

As you do so, prioritize your authenticity, speak your truth, create new boundaries, and ultimately reinforce your commitment to your Ori (Higher Self). Sometimes, we just need to pause and prioritize Self and Source to find the answers.

When you pivot your perspective to process your truth, you may realize that the answers have been clear all along. You may feel a sense of relief in your soul even though your mind may feel worry about the repercussions of expressing said truth. As always, the choice is yours. If you choose for others, do that willingly and accept the inner turmoil that may bring, especially in the long run. Should you choose for yourself, do that knowingly and accept the outer turmoil that may bring, especially in the short term. Choose wisely, or don't choose at all.

Soul Inquiry:

What questions arise as you process a perceived dilemma you are facing right now?

Soul Work:

Visualize the choice you would make if you didn't have to consider anyone else. How does that make you feel? Visualize being honest with others about that choice. How does that make you feel? You know what to do.

ChakRA Activation:

Solar Plexus - Manipura - Ram - I Do - Yellow - 528 Hz - Citrine

TIMING IS DIVINE

"Timing is divine, for it is all already mine."

The concept of time is solely of this world, and we are constantly working our magick in multiple realms simultaneously. As a result, we have to keep in mind that there is no way to know precisely when or if all our wishes will become reality. When we expect everything to go according to our timeline, we set ourselves up to feel a lack of patience. What is for us cannot miss us, but the frequency of impatience can delay it. We exist in a dimension that takes longer for things to present in tangible form, and accepting that is fundamental to appreciating and allowing divine timing. There can only be harvest when our bounty is ripe, and that readiness is determined by nature, not by how hungry we are. To alleviate the impatience, we can plant more seeds, which will also help us acknowledge and appreciate the productivity of what has already grown.

We emit an energy of ingratitude every time we complain about progress being too slow, and that attitude puts a pause on the momentum of our plans. Our linear perception of time may interpret things as moving slowly, but we risk being stagnant when we welcome frustration. Instead, focus on the curves of life and all that you have already attained. Manifest your moments and trust the process. We must submit and surrender to Self and Source to send a clear message to The Creator and our Spirit Team that we believe they got us. Putting your complete trust in them makes it easier to realize that nothing can come before its time and that you are exactly where you are supposed to be. With faith, gratitude, and patience, you will never forget that everything meant for you is already yours.

Soul Inquiry:

How has choosing patience served you in the past?

Soul Work:

Write a list of all the revelations and rewards you received in divine time.

ChakRA Activation:

Heart - Anahata - Yam - I Love - Green - 639 Hz - Green Aventurine

SACRED SACRIFICE

*"I accept what I need to sacrifice
for the highest good of all."*

We will encounter things and people that may only be for a temporary experience or a specific purpose. We often expect to have everything we think we want, but Spirit always knows what we need. We can also hone in on a desire that can lead us to misinterpret a dynamic and engage in a way that does not align with the highest good. We often get signs but ignore what we don't want to accept and rationalize our decisions because it is what we want at the moment. When we receive the messages that express the need to pivot, we must prepare ourselves to be obedient to that guidance to avoid unfortunate consequences. It is always more challenging to obey when it opposes what feels good and even serendipitous. We may question why we would be presented with something that could feel so meant to be and then get messages to the contrary, but those are instances that are most opportune for practicing sacred sacrifice.

It is a precarious position when we feel forced to give something or someone up to serve the greater good because it feels confusing and unfair. Still, as time goes on, we will see that the sacrifice also benefits us. Be gentle and patient with yourself during the challenging moments, especially when you lament or struggle with being obedient. Taking steps forward, backward, left, and right are all part of life's dance, but every move has repercussions. Spirit gives us grace as we choreograph this human experience, but never lose sight of the harmony that will surely come once the sacred sacrifice is made.

Soul Inquiry:

What or who could you let go of that would benefit you and others you care about?

Soul Work:

Write a list of the necessary adjustments you should make and start implementing them today.

ChakRA Activation:

Throat - Vishuddha - Ham - I Speak - Blue - 741 Hz - Turquoise

APPENDIX

1 - Awareness of Oneness p. 21

Our *true tribe* are those who inspire our lives in soulful ways and who we can be our true selves with. We may recognize them on a soul level, so we treat them with a version of love, respect, and care that is sacred, and they, in turn, mirror our harmonious intentions. We don't get to choose our families and the traditional meaning of "tribe," so there may be personalities among us that we don't feel a kinship with despite the relation. I distinguish with the term *true tribe* since they are the unique souls we choose because they show up consistently, authentically and without judgement, whether we are related or not. Allow those healthy dynamics to inspire how you treat everyone.

2 - Divine Duality p. 24

Many of us subscribe to the idea of alter egos that can help us comprehend and navigate our opposing energies. The key to managing our alters is objectively observing our thoughts, feelings, words, and deeds without judging them. That will allow logic to permeate potentially extreme emotions, which can lead us to make more balanced choices.

3 - The Power of Three p. 27

Many religious and sacred symbols, including The Ankh, The Cross, and The Triquetra, represent the power of three energy. "Charmed Ones" refers to three sisters or divine feminine family members who are stronger when they join forces to manifest. Honor your trinity alignments because they have the greatest potential to make tangible magick.

4 - Four Walls of Manifesting p. 30

Spirit always wants to deliver, but often gets mixed signals because of the confusion in our vibrational frequencies. Distractions can dilute the clarity of our intentions, so it is important to distinguish between our needs and wants to prioritize our power's potency.

5 - Winds of Change p. 33

That is when the caterpillar liquifies into the butterfly. It is the lotus growing out of mud. It is the phoenix rising from the ashes. None of these transformations sound pleasant, but we must alter our perception that change should only come easily and without inconvenience.

6 - Sixth Sensing p. 36

As a clairaudient, I can humbly attest to the clear distinction between when I *hear* guidance versus when I *listen* to it. We are all works in progress, but the more we *listen* to our sixth sense, the more access we will have to the cosmic counsel present to guide us. Obedience is an offering.

7 - Perfectly Made p. 39

Some religions teach us that we are imperfect and condition us to believe that we were born with sin and unworthy to receive The Creator, but those are the same dogmas that teach us that The Creator is outside of us. Our divine spark of perfection was placed at the core of our souls by Source, and no human experience could ever separate us from it. Our souls aren't even ours to sell, but some worldly choices can cause us to dim our spark and turn our backs to the light. It's never too late to turn around.

8 - Infinite Abundance p. 42

Abundance absolutely does refer to money, and money is energy like everything else. For that reason, we should always thank our money when we circulate it and give thanks for it returning to us eightfold. That abundance affirmation creates an infinite boomerang effect to ensure our infinite supply of financial abundance.

9 - Embracing Endings p. 45

When we change our perspective of endings, many of us may be able to admit that we would take the "loss" all over again for what we gained in its place.

10 - God Within p. 48

We may not experience everything we are trying to manifest because not everything we think we want is meant for us. The key is to not get discouraged when something doesn't happen the way we want it to. That will help us stay high vibrational so we can be guided towards what we are meant to experience. Being grateful for gratitude refers to being thankful that you acknowledge the manifesting vibration of gratitude. Many people take things for granted, which limits their receptive mode.

11 - Youniversal Laws p. 51

If astrology resonates with you, exploring your birth chart to see how tangibly you are the youniverse is enlightening. It is essential to know the date, location, and exact time of your birth to get the full scope of your birth chart. That way, you will know the precise energies that preside over you and your experiences. There will be a plethora of daunting information, especially if you are new to astrology, so I suggest initially focusing on researching your rising/ascendant sign, sun sign, moon sign, north node, and houses based on the whole sign house system. A personal astrologer would be a valuable resource to help you navigate, but information is widely available online.

12 - Ancestral Alignment p. 54

Those who oppress will always worry that the oppressed will reconnect to a power beyond this realm to restore balance, which is why they have to condition society to denounce ancestral worship. Since we are one with our ancestors, we must show our *transitioned tribe* respect and treat ourselves and each other with the same respect. Ancestral alignment should also inspire us to carry ourselves in a way that will make future generations regard us when we transition from this current life. Live the way you wish to be remembered. I also referred to the Motherland as what is commonly known as Africa, but I would be remiss not to mention her original name, Alkebulan. Knowing the true names and titles that our ancestors used for people and places empowers their legacy and our alignment with them.

13 - Maintain Boundaries p. 57

Many people who cross our boundaries may be unaware of it or unintentionally be causing difficulty because it has never been brought to their attention. That is why speaking up is vital to advocate for yourself and to enlighten the other person in a way that can improve all of their relationships. There are also occasions when we don't say anything because of how someone negatively reacted in the past. Some people can purposely punish those who attempt to advocate for themselves in various abusive ways. They could gaslight, yell, patronize, disrespect, demean, manipulate, give the silent treatment, withhold affection, abandon, and some people get violent. Any of us who have been on the receiving end of that are hesitant to subject ourselves to it again, but rejection is protection. Those reactions are the proof we need to know that it is time to stand our ground or walk away.

14 - Regard Your Regrets p. 60

Reflection also allows us to be honest about a perceived regret to make sure it is something we genuinely are not proud of versus it being about an obligation or someone else's expectation. Not being true to ourselves to appease another should be our only true regret. Once that distinction is made, forgive yourself for a choice you made when you didn't know better and celebrate yourself because now you do. Give thanks for the process and all that it helped you learn about yourself, and release any remnant guilt and shame. Guilt and shame are two of the lowest vibrations that block our blessings even more than any decision we perceive as a regret.

15 - Roots and Fruits p. 63

We should keep in mind that roots grow under the surface of the soil, so you will not see what is initially being formed and transformed. That is where our faith can be fortified because although the roots are not visible, we believe they are growing and that it is only a matter of time before we will savor the sweetest fruits. Likewise, your aspirations must expand to the depths of your soul before they can sprout through the surface. So, nurture that expansion by being in consistent cosmic communion with patience and purpose.

16 - Signed. Sealed. Delivered p. 66

Words carry energy, not only based on etymology, definition, and language, but also based on how we use them — individually, collectively, and historically. Much like the Akashic records, each phrase can manifest a phase that is recorded and cannot be undone and will be a part of your history and your karma. The automatic activation in your written word can create or destroy — just as our spoken words, thoughts, feelings, and actions can — so hold your pen like a wand and script words of miracles over your life and the world. Your wish is your command.

17 - Too Sacred To Share p. 69

Some things are just for you and are meant to be a personal message or occurrence that is more potent if kept private. These sacred experiences can come in the form of relationships, ideas, lucid dreams, downloads, celestial encounters, ambitions, visions, etc. The more honored and emotionally overwhelmed you feel by the experience, the more you should keep it to yourself. As you guard it with reverence, you will become clearer on how to proceed with the information.

18 - Sovereign Soul p. 72

You will receive more clarity and favor when you clear the programming you have been practicing and perfecting based on what serves the system's agenda. This deprogramming is necessary for the macro and micro lenses of life. Speaking the associated declaration for this *cosmic concept* daily is a powerful way to reinforce your soul sovereignty, along with declaring that you **do not consent** to any ill intentions that attempt to threaten your freedom.

19 - Water Works p. 75

Water is a feminine principle that aligns with emotions, intuition, birthing something new, and washing away debris, which helps put us in receiving mode. Connecting with water goddesses of various traditions assists in the acceleration of your aspirations. Watering your plants is a simple way to pour libation in honor of our ancestors and Earth Mother. It is a cathartic and foundational method of offering that unifies the feminine elements of water and Earth to will waves of abundance. Just as water provides what the Earth needs to ensure a harvest, water the seeds you want Spirit to make fruitful. We have the power to charge the permeating element of water by infusing it with the energies of herbs, fruits, flowers, essential oils, tinctures, salt, honey, crystals, the moon, and the sun, which can magnify your magick even more. Adding those activated elixirs and rainwater to your bath creates a "Self-Love Soak" that assists in the symbolic soaking up of your intentions. Spring water is ideal to use for elixirs, and exposing your water to sound frequencies will allow the water to absorb those vibrations and enhance its manifesting power.

20 - Burn Baby Burn p. 78

Fire is a masculine principle that aligns with creativity, passion, willpower, and burning away what no longer serves to help encourage inspired action. Connecting with fire gods of various traditions assists in the acceleration of your aspirations. Fire rituals are a fervent and ascending method of offering that unifies with air — its co-masculine element — as we observe the smoke being carried up to the energies above. Oxygen spreads a forest fire, so breathe life into what you want Spirit to fuel. Much like erupted lava creates the most fertile soil, be grateful for all that is about to grow. Candle magick is another fire ritual that can be customized for a specific outcome based on the candle's intention, color, inscription, or how it is fixed or anointed. After cleansing your candle, you can burn items in your candle's flame, adorn your candle with crystals and other fireproof decor, or place written petitions underneath your candle before lighting it. Be sure to use fireproof vessels and votives when burning anything, especially candles, and keep them away from anything flammable. Do not leave incense, resin, or candles burning unattended or overnight, and don't blow them out with your breath. Smother flames with a candle snuffer because using the power of your breath can extinguish your intentions along with the flame. I also don't advise using matches in your home to light anything. Matches contain sulfur, which could attract low vibrational energies that can interfere with your auspicious intentions.

21 - Exhale. Inhale. Exhale p. 81

Air is a masculine principle that aligns with intellect, change, the unseen, and blowing away unstable energy, which helps put us in logic mode. Connecting with air gods of various traditions assists in the acceleration of your aspirations. Breathwork is imperative and beneficial to our mind, body, heart, and soul alignment, and it can relax, energize, or inspire joy. While performing the introduced breath exercise, with every exhale, hold your hands up to your mouth to feel the coolness of the air on your hands as you visualize everything that no longer serves you being released with your breath. With every inhale, visualize bringing in everything you desire that has that whole space to take up.

22 - Sole II Soil p. 84

Earth is a feminine principle that aligns with grounding, stability, fertility, and burying the old, which helps put us in nurture mode. Connecting with earth goddesses of various traditions assists in the acceleration of your aspirations. Since grounding and other outdoor activities may be a seasonal experience, depending on the climate of your location, grounding items that can be purchased for indoor use all year round also include grounding socks, shoes, and bedsheets. They provide alignment with the natural electric field of Earth Mother. They also assist in protecting you from EMF and harmful radiation, so are ideal to use when working on devices such as your phone or computer.

23 - Back II Natural p. 87

This was the first *cosmic concept* that inspired me to spell what should be "to" with two letter I's (II/

ii) in homage to the Rastafari concept of I & I, which reminds us that we are not separate from each other, The Creator, or nature. Nature-based practices like grounding, tree-hugging, sun/moon worship, growing our own food, reducing our carbon footprint, plant-based eating, and fasting are all ways to remind ourselves that we are one with nature. Giving thanks to your herbs for their healing when cooking and making tea will magnify their medicinal properties and help you absorb their nutrients more. Bay leaves are especially powerful for manifesting and magick. Getting back II natural also reminds us that trees, flowers, plants, animals, birds, and insects are sentient beings, which should make it that much easier for us to be more aware and sensitive to our flora and fauna family. They, too, provide us with insightful messages and cosmic confirmations. Learning more about the Yoruba Forces of Nature, known as The Òrìṣà/Orisha, can deepen your inner-standing of nature. You will be transformed by how tangibly every natural occurrence can protect you and infuse your intentions.

24 - Release II Increase p. 90

Stagnation occurs from holding on to who and what no longer serves us. It blocks our blessings and reinforces internal and external obstacles to everything we say we want. A scarcity mentality leads us towards the desire to acquire and accumulate, often based on quantity versus quality. We also frequently don't acknowledge our personal growth enough, which causes our new sense of self to stay committed to a choice made by an older version of ourselves. Oftentimes, this is prevalent in our personal relationships once we are honest about the people who are still around us, yet have not grown with us. We put our prosperity on pause every time we prioritize pessimistic people. Once we are aware of this, it is up to us to choose to prolong the problem. Cutting unhealthy earthly bondages also makes it easier to free ourselves from etheric bonds from present and past lives. It is imperative to fortify our faith to know that we are worthy of the more in store so that we can close any deficient door. Working with the moon is a powerful way to align with release to increase frequencies. Full moons are ideal for release energy, which can be accompanied by cord-cutting practices and fire and air rituals. New moons are ideal for increase energy, which can be accompanied by creative practices and earth and water rituals. Working with a Rose of Jericho (Resurrection Plant) is also powerful. Water it during the new moon phase and allow it to dry and close during the full moon phase to resurrect all stagnant energies meant to thrive in your life.

25 - Feel It II Heal It p. 93

Start with the heart. The heart chakRA is the most crucial energy center to work on keeping balanced when on an emotional healing journey, especially because it is the center chakRA. When in balance, it helps the other chakRAs stay in alignment; as above, so below. Likewise, when the heart chakRA is wounded, we can feel an overall sense of instability. Allowing yourself to genuinely feel your uncomfortable emotions is the first step to getting your heart chakRA in balance. Meditating and sleeping to heart chakRA sound frequencies is a powerful added support that helps you heal on a subconscious level.

26 - Face It II Replace It p. 96

Being honest about who and what we need to replace requires courage and fortitude because making those changes is internal work and has nothing to do with anyone else. We cannot change others; we can only change ourselves. We also can't force anyone to acknowledge how we have changed, especially because they are less likely to recognize it if they have remained the same. It is a misuse and abuse of our energy trying to convince someone of something they don't want to believe. Most people who deny your growth because of their stagnancy also have a subconscious aversion to the new version of you, which may require you to move away from the relationship for your own protection.

27 - Eye See You p. 99

Be mindful when working with "spiritual advisors" who emphasize the presence of negative energies around you. Be especially cautious based on their suggested protocol and how they will benefit from your fear, especially financially. As a healing facilitator, I make it a point to not disclose details of negative forces when I detect them because it is counterproductive to instill fear in someone when I am trying to help them raise their vibration. I instead just share whatever release rituals are required. Their energetic augment will also assist in their protection and peace of mind, which is most effective in clearing and blocking any negative influences. For portable and consistent protection, you can make a saltwater mist to carry with you to spray over your head and body any time the energy feels unsettling. You can also wear protective talismans like the Nazar and the Hamsa and crystals like Black Obsidian, Black Tourmaline, Smoky Quartz, Clear Quartz, Gold Tiger's Eye, and Lapis Lazuli.

28 - Mirror Work p. 102

Mirror work can be an emotionally intense exercise, so be sure to give yourself enough private time to feel relaxed and safe. Cry if you feel compelled to; don't hold it in. Your salty tears will be cathartic and serve as a tangible release from anything holding you back from seeing your full splendor. The process can often feel like an out-of-body experience, so it is helpful and enlightening to audio or video record yourself so you can listen back to it. Listening to your own words will resonate on a deeper level, and it will be powerful to have those vulnerable and revealing moments to refer back to throughout your healing journey.

29 - Growing Pains p. 105

Most of us underestimate what we are capable of, and it is more often through strain that we realize our true strength and unlimited potential. We may also lose people on our journey when we choose to grow and go in a different direction. These tower moments of unexpected upheaval and sudden change teach us what grief feels like, and we have a choice to stay curled up in a ball of rubble or get up and start again through the pain that will pass.

30 - Shadow & Shine p. 108

Low vibrational frequencies like guilt and shame only spiral us into feeling like we are not worthy of grace or forgiveness. Choosing to be gentle with ourselves in the face of being responsible for a choice that affected us or others harmfully is challenging, but necessary. We may not always do the "right" thing— which could stem from many reasons — but ultimately, anyone is capable of anything when dealing with unprecedented conditions in unchartered territory. We are divine beings living human experiences, so don't punish yourself or others for the duality. Self-study refers to how we can research our personalities, archetypes, and subtle bodies through intangible and tangible resources. Prayer, meditation, silence, breathwork, and ancestral alignment are some effective intangible ways to uncover personal energetic information. Tangible resources can include exploring your astrological birth chart, numerology, human design, and online questionnaires such as the Myers Briggs personality test and other quizzes to discover your love language, aura color, spiral dynamics, and more.

31 - There Are No Dilemmas p. 111

Some questions that may help you navigate a perceived dilemma are as follows: Do I feel a sense of obligation to someone that I am not actually responsible for? Do I have doubts about a decision I made? Do I feel differently about someone or something? Why do I feel guilty about being honest? Am I being true to myself? Can I live with myself if I make this choice? Dig deep, be honest, and prepare for your outer reality to reflect your inner truth.

32 - Timing Is Divine p. 114

We risk our alignment and manifestations when we send messages to our Spirit Team that indicate we don't trust that they know what they are doing. We don't do this intentionally, disrespectfully, or blatantly. Still, unfortunately, it is as simple and subtle as how we choose to feel. Impatience, frustration, doubt, fear, ingratitude, anger, annoyance, and aggravation are some emotions we feel when things don't go "our way," which is all it takes to emit a frequency of distrust to the energies we request support from. The answers to our prayers may be on the verge of pouring over us until those low vibrational emotions pinch off the flow from Source. Believe that what is meant for you is right there, no matter how long it takes.

Manifest your moments refers to practicing your power by focusing on what you can transform in the now. There may be a lot that we hope for on the horizon, but we can create so much magick and miracles every second of every day. That daily alignment of being fully present helps us detach from future outcomes, which will ironically manifest them much faster.

33 - Sacred Sacrifice p. 117

We understand the meaning of sacrifice through certain relationships and religions — like a mother who sacrifices her body to carry, birth, and breastfeed her child, a tradition that requires giving offerings in exchange for an answered petition, or prophets and people who have martyred themselves for a holy mission or message. That kind of energy exchange is a sacred and bittersweet act that we can feel when we have to surrender something or someone we wish to secure.

Sacred Soul Simplified

Some sacred space to simplify your sacred soul

Cosmic Concept Title: _____
Cosmic Concept Number: _____
ChakRA Activation: _____

Soul Inquiry:

_____
_____
_____
_____
_____
_____
_____
_____
_____
_____

Soul Work:

_____
_____
_____
_____
_____
_____
_____
_____
_____
_____
_____

Additional Notes:

_____
_____
_____
_____

Sacred Soul Simplified

Some sacred space to simplify your sacred soul

Cosmic Concept Title: _____
Cosmic Concept Number: _____
ChakRA Activation: _____

Soul Inquiry:

_____
_____
_____
_____
_____
_____
_____
_____
_____

Soul Work:

_____
_____
_____
_____
_____
_____
_____
_____
_____
_____

Additional Notes:

_____
_____
_____
_____

Sacred Soul Simplified

Some sacred space to simplify your sacred soul

Cosmic Concept Title: _____
Cosmic Concept Number: _____
ChakRA Activation: _____

Soul Inquiry:

_____
_____
_____
_____
_____
_____
_____
_____
_____
_____

Soul Work:

_____
_____
_____
_____
_____
_____
_____
_____
_____
_____

Additional Notes:

_____
_____
_____
_____

Sacred Soul Simplified

Some sacred space to simplify your sacred soul

Cosmic Concept Title: _____
Cosmic Concept Number: _____
ChakRA Activation: _____

Soul Inquiry:

_____
_____
_____
_____
_____
_____
_____
_____
_____

Soul Work:

_____
_____
_____
_____
_____
_____
_____
_____
_____
_____

Additional Notes:

_____
_____
_____
_____

Sacred Soul Simplified

Some sacred space to simplify your sacred soul

Cosmic Concept Title: _____

Cosmic Concept Number: _____

ChakRA Activation: _____

Soul Inquiry:

_____
_____
_____
_____
_____
_____
_____
_____
_____
_____

Soul Work:

_____
_____
_____
_____
_____
_____
_____
_____
_____
_____

Additional Notes:

_____
_____
_____
_____

Sacred Soul Simplified

Some sacred space to simplify your sacred soul

Cosmic Concept Title: _____

Cosmic Concept Number: _____

ChakRA Activation: _____

Soul Inquiry:

_____
_____
_____
_____
_____
_____
_____
_____
_____
_____

Soul Work:

_____
_____
_____
_____
_____
_____
_____
_____
_____
_____

Additional Notes:

_____
_____
_____
_____

Sacred Soul Simplified

Some sacred space to simplify your sacred soul

Cosmic Concept Title: _____
Cosmic Concept Number: _____
ChakRA Activation: _____

Soul Inquiry:

_____
_____
_____
_____
_____
_____
_____
_____
_____
_____

Soul Work:

_____
_____
_____
_____
_____
_____
_____
_____
_____
_____

Additional Notes:

_____
_____
_____
_____

Sacred Soul Simplified

Some sacred space to simplify your sacred soul

Cosmic Concept Title: _____
Cosmic Concept Number: _____
ChakRA Activation: _____

Soul Inquiry:

_____
_____
_____
_____
_____
_____
_____
_____
_____
_____

Soul Work:

_____
_____
_____
_____
_____
_____
_____
_____
_____
_____

Additional Notes:

_____
_____
_____
_____

Sacred Soul Simplified

Some sacred space to simplify your sacred soul

Cosmic Concept Title: _____
Cosmic Concept Number: _____
ChakRA Activation: _____

Soul Inquiry:

_____
_____
_____
_____
_____
_____
_____
_____
_____

Soul Work:

_____
_____
_____
_____
_____
_____
_____
_____
_____
_____

Additional Notes:

_____
_____
_____
_____

Sacred Soul Simplified

Some sacred space to simplify your sacred soul

Cosmic Concept Title: _____
Cosmic Concept Number: _____
ChakRA Activation: _____

Soul Inquiry:

_____
_____
_____
_____
_____
_____
_____
_____
_____
_____

Soul Work:

_____
_____
_____
_____
_____
_____
_____
_____
_____
_____

Additional Notes:

_____
_____
_____
_____

Sacred Soul Simplified

Some sacred space to simplify your sacred soul

Cosmic Concept Title: _____
Cosmic Concept Number: _____
ChakRA Activation: _____

Soul Inquiry:

_____
_____
_____
_____
_____
_____
_____
_____
_____
_____

Soul Work:

_____
_____
_____
_____
_____
_____
_____
_____
_____
_____

Additional Notes:

_____
_____
_____
_____

Sacred Soul Simplified

Some sacred space to simplify your sacred soul

Cosmic Concept Title: _____
Cosmic Concept Number: _____
ChakRA Activation: _____

Soul Inquiry:

_____
_____
_____
_____
_____
_____
_____
_____
_____
_____

Soul Work:

_____
_____
_____
_____
_____
_____
_____
_____
_____
_____

Additional Notes:

_____
_____
_____
_____

Sacred Soul Simplified

Some sacred space to simplify your sacred soul

Cosmic Concept Title: _____
Cosmic Concept Number: _____
ChakRA Activation: _____

Soul Inquiry:

_____
_____
_____
_____
_____
_____
_____
_____
_____
_____

Soul Work:

_____
_____
_____
_____
_____
_____
_____
_____
_____
_____

Additional Notes:

_____
_____
_____
_____

Sacred Soul Simplified

Some sacred space to simplify your sacred soul

Cosmic Concept Title: _____
Cosmic Concept Number: _____
ChakRA Activation: _____

Soul Inquiry:

_____
_____
_____
_____
_____
_____
_____
_____
_____

Soul Work:

_____
_____
_____
_____
_____
_____
_____
_____
_____
_____

Additional Notes:

_____
_____
_____
_____

Sacred Soul Simplified

Some sacred space to simplify your sacred soul

Cosmic Concept Title: _____
Cosmic Concept Number: _____
ChakRA Activation: _____

Soul Inquiry:

_____
_____
_____
_____
_____
_____
_____
_____

Soul Work:

_____
_____
_____
_____
_____
_____
_____
_____

Additional Notes:

_____
_____
_____
_____

Sacred Soul Simplified

Some sacred space to simplify your sacred soul

Cosmic Concept Title: _____

Cosmic Concept Number: _____

ChakRA Activation: _____

Soul Inquiry:

_____
_____
_____
_____
_____
_____
_____
_____
_____
_____

Soul Work:

_____
_____
_____
_____
_____
_____
_____
_____
_____
_____

Additional Notes:

_____
_____
_____
_____

Sacred Soul Simplified

Some sacred space to simplify your sacred soul

Cosmic Concept Title: _____
Cosmic Concept Number: _____
ChakRA Activation: _____

Soul Inquiry:

_____
_____
_____
_____
_____
_____
_____
_____
_____
_____

Soul Work:

_____
_____
_____
_____
_____
_____
_____
_____
_____
_____

Additional Notes:

_____
_____
_____
_____

Sacred Soul Simplified

Some sacred space to simplify your sacred soul

Cosmic Concept Title: _____
Cosmic Concept Number: _____
ChakRA Activation: _____

Soul Inquiry:

_____
_____
_____
_____
_____
_____
_____
_____
_____
_____

Soul Work:

_____
_____
_____
_____
_____
_____
_____
_____
_____
_____
_____

Additional Notes:

_____
_____
_____
_____

Sacred Soul Simplified

Some sacred space to simplify your sacred soul

Cosmic Concept Title: _____
Cosmic Concept Number: _____
ChakRA Activation: _____

Soul Inquiry:

_____
_____
_____
_____
_____
_____
_____
_____
_____
_____

Soul Work:

_____
_____
_____
_____
_____
_____
_____
_____
_____
_____

Additional Notes:

_____
_____
_____
_____

Sacred Soul Simplified

Some sacred space to simplify your sacred soul

Cosmic Concept Title: _____
Cosmic Concept Number: _____
ChakRA Activation: _____

Soul Inquiry:

_____
_____
_____
_____
_____
_____
_____
_____
_____

Soul Work:

_____
_____
_____
_____
_____
_____
_____
_____
_____
_____

Additional Notes:

_____
_____
_____
_____

Sacred Soul Simplified

Some sacred space to simplify your sacred soul

Cosmic Concept Title: _____

Cosmic Concept Number: _____

ChakRA Activation: _____

Soul Inquiry:

_____
_____
_____
_____
_____
_____
_____
_____
_____

Soul Work:

_____
_____
_____
_____
_____
_____
_____
_____
_____

Additional Notes:

_____
_____
_____
_____

Sacred Soul Simplified

Some sacred space to simplify your sacred soul

Cosmic Concept Title: _____
Cosmic Concept Number: _____
ChakRA Activation: _____

Soul Inquiry:

_____
_____
_____
_____
_____
_____
_____
_____
_____

Soul Work:

_____
_____
_____
_____
_____
_____
_____
_____
_____
_____

Additional Notes:

_____
_____
_____
_____

Sacred Soul Simplified

Some sacred space to simplify your sacred soul

Cosmic Concept Title: _____

Cosmic Concept Number: _____

ChakRA Activation: _____

Soul Inquiry:

_____
_____
_____
_____
_____
_____
_____
_____
_____
_____

Soul Work:

_____
_____
_____
_____
_____
_____
_____
_____
_____
_____

Additional Notes:

_____
_____
_____
_____

Sacred Soul Simplified

Some sacred space to simplify your sacred soul

Cosmic Concept Title: _____
Cosmic Concept Number: _____
ChakRA Activation: _____

Soul Inquiry:

_____
_____
_____
_____
_____
_____
_____
_____
_____
_____

Soul Work:

_____
_____
_____
_____
_____
_____
_____
_____
_____
_____

Additional Notes:

_____
_____
_____
_____

Sacred Soul Simplified

Some sacred space to simplify your sacred soul

Cosmic Concept Title: _____
Cosmic Concept Number: _____
ChakRA Activation: _____

Soul Inquiry:

_____
_____
_____
_____
_____
_____
_____
_____
_____
_____

Soul Work:

_____
_____
_____
_____
_____
_____
_____
_____
_____
_____

Additional Notes:

_____
_____
_____
_____

Sacred Soul Simplified

Some sacred space to simplify your sacred soul

Cosmic Concept Title: _____

Cosmic Concept Number: _____

ChakRA Activation: _____

Soul Inquiry:

_____
_____
_____
_____
_____
_____
_____
_____
_____
_____

Soul Work:

_____
_____
_____
_____
_____
_____
_____
_____
_____
_____

Additional Notes:

_____
_____
_____
_____

Sacred Soul Simplified

Some sacred space to simplify your sacred soul

Cosmic Concept Title: _____

Cosmic Concept Number: _____

ChakRA Activation: _____

Soul Inquiry:

_____
_____
_____
_____
_____
_____
_____
_____
_____

Soul Work:

_____
_____
_____
_____
_____
_____
_____
_____
_____

Additional Notes:

_____
_____
_____
_____

Sacred Soul Simplified

Some sacred space to simplify your sacred soul

Cosmic Concept Title: _____

Cosmic Concept Number: _____

ChakRA Activation: _____

Soul Inquiry:

_____
_____
_____
_____
_____
_____
_____
_____
_____
_____

Soul Work:

_____
_____
_____
_____
_____
_____
_____
_____
_____
_____
_____

Additional Notes:

_____
_____
_____
_____

Sacred Soul Simplified

Some sacred space to simplify your sacred soul

Cosmic Concept Title: _____
Cosmic Concept Number: _____
ChakRA Activation: _____

Soul Inquiry:

_____
_____
_____
_____
_____
_____
_____
_____
_____
_____

Soul Work:

_____
_____
_____
_____
_____
_____
_____
_____
_____
_____

Additional Notes:

_____
_____
_____
_____

Sacred Soul Simplified

Some sacred space to simplify your sacred soul

Cosmic Concept Title: _____
Cosmic Concept Number: _____
ChakRA Activation: _____

Soul Inquiry:

_____
_____
_____
_____
_____
_____
_____
_____
_____
_____

Soul Work:

_____
_____
_____
_____
_____
_____
_____
_____
_____
_____

Additional Notes:

_____
_____
_____
_____